World Languages

Families in
Italian

Daniel Nunn

Raintree is an imprint of Capstone Global Library Limited, a company incorporated in England and Wales having its registered office at 7 Pilgrim Street, London, EC4V 6LB - Registered company number: 6695582

To contact Raintree please phone 0845 6044371, fax + 44 (0) 1865 312263, or email: myorders@raintreepublishers.co.uk. Customers from outside the UK please telephone +44 1865 312262.

Edited by Daniel Nunn, Rebecca Rissman & Sian Smith
Designed by Joanna Hinton-Malivoire
Picture research by Tracy Cummins
Production by Victoria Fitzgerald
Originated by Capstone Global Library Ltd
Printed and bound in China by Leo Paper Products Ltd

ISBN 978 1 406 25089 3
16 15 14 13 12
10 9 8 7 6 5 4 3 2 1

British Library Cataloguing in Publication Data
Nunn, Daniel.
Families in Italian: le famiglie. – (World languages. Families)
1. Italian language–Vocabulary–Pictorial works–Juvenile literature. 2. Families–Italy–Terminology–Pictorial works–Juvenile literature.
I. Title II. Series
  458.1-dc23

Acknowledgements
We would like to thank the following for permission to reproduce photographs: Shutterstock pp.4 (Catalin Petolea), 5 (optimarc), 5, 6 (Petrenko Andriy), 5, 7 (Tyler Olson), 5, 8 (Andrey Shadrin), 9 (Erika Cross), 10 (Alena Brozova), 5, 11 (Maxim Petrichuk), 12 (auremar), 13 (Mika Heittola), 5, 14, 15 (Alexander Raths), 5, 16 (Samuel Borges), 17 (Vitalii Nesterchuk), 18 (pat138241), 19 (Fotokostic), 20 (Cheryl Casey), 21 (spotmatik).

Cover photographs of two women and a man reproduced with permission of Shutterstock (Yuri Arcurs). Cover photograph of a girl reproduced with permission of istockphoto (© Sean Lockes). Back cover photograph of a girl reproduced with permission of Shutterstock (Erika Cross).

We would like to thank Nino Puma, Joan Parker, and Paola Bisicchia for their invaluable help in the preparation of this book.

Every effort has been made to contact copyright holders of material reproduced in this book. Any omissions will be rectified in subsequent printings if notice is given to the publisher.

Contents

Ciao!

Mi chiamo Daniel.

My name is Daniel.

4

E questa è la mia famiglia.

And this is my family.

Mia madre e mio padre

mia madre

Questa è mia madre.

This is my mother.

mio padre

Questo è mio padre.

This is my father.

Mio fratello e mia sorella

mio fratello

Questo è mio fratello.

This is my brother.

Questa è mia sorella.

This is my sister.

La mia matrigna e il mio patrigno

la mia matrigna

Questa è la mia matrigna.

This is my step-mother.

Questo è il mio patrigno.

This is my step-father.

Il mio fratellastro e la mia sorellastra

il mio fratellastro

Questo è il mio fratellastro.

This is my step-brother.

la mia sorellastra

Questa è la mia sorellastra.

This is my step-sister.

Mia nonna e mio nonno

mia nonna

Questa è mia nonna.

This is my grandmother.

Questo è mio nonno.

This is my grandfather.

Mia zia e mio zio

mia zia

Questa è mia zia.

This is my aunt.

mio zio

Questo è mio zio.

This is my uncle.

I miei cugini

mia cugina

Questi sono i miei cugini.

These are my cousins.

mio cugino

19

I miei amici

la mia amica

Questi sono i miei amici.

These are my friends.

il mio amico

Dictionary

Italian word	How to say it	English word
amica	ah-mee-kah	friend (female)
amici	ah-mee-chee	friends
amico	ah-mee-koh	friend (male)
ciao	ch-owh	hi
cugina	koo-gee-nah	cousin (female)
cugini	koo-gee-nee	cousins
cugino	koo-gee-noh	cousin (male)
e	ay	and
famiglia	fa-mee-lia	family
fratellastro	fra-tell-last-ro	step-brother
fratello	fra-tell-lo	brother
i	ee	the (plural)
il	eel	the (male singular)
la	lah	the (female singular)
madre	mah-dreh	mother
matrigna	mah-treen-ya	step-mother

Italian word	How to say it	English word
mi chiamo	me kee-ah-moh	my name is
mia	mee-ah	my (female singular)
miei	mee-ay-ee	my (plural)
mio	mee-oh	my (male singular)
nonna	non-nah	grandmother
nonno	non-no	grandfather
padre	pa-dreh	father
patrigno	pah-treen-yo	step-father
questa è	koo-est-ah ay	this is (female)
questi sono	koo-est-ee soh-no	these are
questo è	koo-est-oh ay	this is (male)
sorella	so-rell-la	sister
sorellastra	so-rell-last-ra	step-sister
zia	zee-ah	aunt
zio	zee-oh	uncle

See words in the "How to say it" columns for a rough guide to pronunciations.

Index

Notes for parents and teachers

In Italian, nouns are either masculine or feminine. The word for 'my' changes accordingly – either 'mio' (masculine) or 'mia' (feminine). Sometimes nouns have different spellings too, which is why the word for 'cousin' can be spelled either 'cugino' (male) or 'cugina' (female).

'Questi sono' appears in the Dictionary on page 23 as 'these are'. This is the masculine plural form. The feminine plural form doesn't appear in the book but it is 'queste sono' (pronounced 'koo-est-tay sohno'). Similarly 'amici' means a mixture of male and female friends (plural). It doesn't appear in the book but for female friends, the plural 'amiche' is used. Similarly, 'I' and 'miei' are translated in the dictionary as 'the' and 'my' respectively: these are the masculine plural forms, and can be used to refer to a mixture of female and male friends. The feminine plural forms are 'le' and 'mie' respectively.

Due to the way some sentences are constructed in Italian, if you translate these directly using the dictionary, the phrase 'the my' will appear. In these cases we don't include the definite articles when we translate, so the word 'the' should be left out. For example 'Questi sono i miei amici' should be translated as 'These are my friends' rather than 'These are the my friends'.